ANGRY earth

TERRIFYING TORNADOES

By Kristen Rajczak

Gareth Stevens
Publishing

Please visit our website, www.garethstevens.com. For a free color catalog of all our high-quality books, call toll free 1-800-542-2595 or fax 1-877-542-2596.

Library of Congress Cataloging-in-Publication Data

Rajczak, Kristen.
Terrifying tornadoes / Kristen Rajczak.
    p. cm. — (Angry earth)
Includes index.
ISBN 978-1-4339-6543-2 (pbk.)
ISBN 978-1-4339-6544-9 (6-pack)
ISBN 978-1-4339-6541-8 (library binding)
1. Tornadoes—Juvenile literature. I. Title.
QC955.2.R35 2012
551.55'3—dc23

                                    2011033650

First Edition

Published in 2012 by
Gareth Stevens Publishing
111 East 14th Street, Suite 349
New York, NY 10003

Copyright © 2012 Gareth Stevens Publishing

Designer: Katelyn E. Reynolds
Editor: Therese Shea

Photo credits: Cover, p. 1 Alan R. Moller/Stone/Getty Images; cover, pp. 1, 3–32 text/image box graphic iStockphoto.com; (cover, pp. 1, 3–32 background and newspaper graphics), pp. 6, 8 (inset), 13 (inset) Shutterstock.com; p. 4 Stephen Myles/AFP/Getty Images; pp. 5 (inset), 18 NOAA/Getty Images; pp. 5 (main), 26–27 Carsten Peter/National Geographic/Getty Images; p. 7 Dorling Kindersley/Getty Images; pp. 8 (main), 10 Harald Richter/AFP/Getty Images; p. 11 Ross Tuckerman/AFP/Getty Images; p. 13 (main) John Sleezer/ Kansas City Star/MCT via Getty Images; p. 14 Robert Laberge/Getty Images; p. 15 Mike Theiss/National Geographic/Getty Images; p. 16 James Alcock/AFP/Getty Images; p. 17 (inset) David McNew/Getty Images; p. 17 (main) Greg Messier/Getty Images; pp. 18–19 Ryan McGinnis/Flickr/Getty Images; p. 21 (inset) Scott Olson/Getty Images; p. 21 (main) DAJ/Getty Images; p. 22 Tom Pennington/Getty Images; p. 23 Nickolas Kamm/AFP/Getty Images; p. 24 Julie Denesha/Getty Images; p. 25 (both) Topical Press Agency/Hulton Archive/Getty Images; pp. 27 (inset), 29 (main) Chris Johns/National Geographic/Getty Images; p. 28 Brett Deering/Getty Images; p. 29 (inset) iStockphoto/Thinkstock.

Printed in the United States of America

CPSIA compliance information: Batch #CW12GS: For further information contact Gareth Stevens, New York, New York at 1-800-542-2595.

CONTENTS

Words in the glossary appear in **bold** type the first time they are used in the text.

WHAT IS A TORNADO?

In most places in the United States, wind speeds usually don't exceed 15 miles (24 km) per hour. The most powerful tornadoes have winds that reach more than 300 miles (483 km) per hour! A tornado is a column of fiercely **rotating** winds that extends from a storm cloud to the ground.

There were 1,282 tornadoes reported in 44 US states in 2010. Tornadoes can cause a lot of harm in a community. They rip up trees and knock down buildings. It's important to know how to be safe during a storm like this. First, let's learn how tornadoes form.

tornado in Italy (2009)

Watches and Warnings

In 1953, the National Weather Service (NWS) began studying, forecasting, and warning the public when a tornado might hit. A tornado watch is issued when an area has conditions that could cause a tornado. A tornado warning is issued when a tornado has been reported.

map tracking
tornado conditions

◁ Tornadoes
are sometimes
called cyclones
or twisters.

About 90 percent of tornadoes form from thunderstorms. Thunderstorms commonly occur when a warm **front** meets a cold front or when a wet air mass meets a dry air mass. Both events push warm, wet air high into the atmosphere. There, moisture in the air **condenses** and creates cumulonimbus clouds, which are thick, tall rain clouds. Cooler air moves in below to replace the rising warm air, resulting in wind.

The storm's strength gathers as the cloud mass grows. Water droplets in the clouds have electrical charges that create lightning and the accompanying thunder. When wind speed increases and wind direction changes, a tornado may form.

Supercell Thunderstorms

Many tornadoes form from supercell thunderstorms. Supercell thunderstorms are those that last longer than an hour. They grow from a leaning, spinning updraft that can be 10 miles (16 km) across and 50,000 feet (15,240 m) tall!

supercell cloud

This is a diagram of a tornado. The movement of air into the upper atmosphere is called an updraft. The cold air traveling down is called a downdraft. Both create wind.

wall cloud

In 1967, **Hurricane** Beulah caused thunderstorms that produced 115 tornadoes in Texas!

8

Changes in wind speed and direction create spinning, **horizontal** winds. The column of warm air angles up into the clouds and begins to spin **vertically**. This huge area of rotating air—called a mesocyclone—can be from 2 to 6 miles (3 to 10 km) wide. Within this area, marked by a mass of low-lying clouds called a wall cloud, tornadoes form.

Tornadoes can also form when a hurricane comes ashore. The powerful winds and great masses of moist air that hurricanes transport can create tornado conditions. Many states along the Gulf of Mexico experience tornadoes just before a hurricane reaches land.

Weak to Violent

Weak Tornadoes
- 69 percent of all tornadoes
- Winds less than 110 miles (177 km) per hour

Strong Tornadoes
- 29 percent of all tornadoes
- Winds 110 to 205 miles (177 to 330 km) per hour

Violent Tornadoes
- 2 percent of all tornadoes
- Winds more than 205 miles (330 km) per hour

THE FUNNEL CLOUD

Do you picture a dark, swirling column of wind when you think of a tornado? This column is called a funnel cloud when it isn't in contact with the ground. At this point, it may also be called a condensation funnel. But it isn't officially called a tornado until it reaches the ground.

Usually, the more water vapor there is in the air and the stronger the winds are, the larger the column will be. However, the look of a funnel cloud changes as it gains and loses power. Some tornadoes can't be seen at all until they pick up dust and **debris**!

tornado in Texas (1995)

Round and Round

Earth's rotation is partly responsible for the way tornadoes turn. Tornadoes are usually cyclonic. That is, they turn counterclockwise in the Northern Hemisphere and clockwise in the Southern Hemisphere. Less than 2 percent of tornadoes are anticyclonic. That means they spin in the opposite direction. Anticyclonic tornadoes form in areas with cool, sinking air.

▲

Funnel clouds range from several feet to many miles across. The size of a tornado isn't always a sign of its strength.

TORNADOES HAPPEN EVERYWHERE

Tornadoes have happened on every continent except Antarctica. By far, the United States is the country with the most tornadoes every year. The tornadoes in the United States are also the strongest and most **destructive** in the world.

Tornadoes have occurred in every US state. They're found in the greatest number and strength in the central part of the country, which is nicknamed Tornado Alley for this reason. This area includes parts of Texas, Oklahoma, Kansas, Nebraska, South Dakota, and Colorado. Florida also has many tornadoes because of the state's high number of thunderstorms, though tornadoes there are generally weaker.

Minnesota Tops 2010

In 2010, Minnesota had more tornadoes than any other state. Of the more than 113 tornadoes that hit Minnesota in 2010, 48 touched down on a single day—June 17. Before this, Minnesota's record for most tornadoes in 1 day had been 27, set in 1992.

Tornado Alley

A resident of Chapman, Kansas, looks for belongings after his home was destroyed by a 2008 tornado.

13

WHEN DO TORNADOES OCCUR?

Tornadoes have been reported every day of the year and at every time of the day. It's easy to understand why **predicting** them is so difficult. However, **meteorologists** keep track of the most common times and dates that tornadoes occur.

Most tornadoes occur in April, May, and June. They happen most often between midafternoon and early evening. The most common time for a tornado to hit is between 5 and 6 p.m. The most violent tornadoes usually form between 6 and 7 p.m. Tornadoes happen least often between 5 and 6 a.m.

two tornadoes in Denver, Colorado (2002)

SKYWARN is the name of a group of people all over the United States trained to watch for dangerous weather such as tornadoes. If they see a funnel cloud forming, they call a special telephone number. Many times, SKYWARN members are police officers and firefighters who have been trained to spot tornadoes. SKYWARN has nearly 290,000 "spotters."

Most tornadoes only last about 2 to 3 minutes. Some last longer, though. The researchers in this photo must be prepared to move fast when tracking a tornado.

TYPES OF TORNADOES

There are several types of tornadoes. Supercell tornadoes form from supercell thunderstorms. These thunderstorms may produce wedge-shaped tornadoes with violent winds that can be more than 200 miles (322 km) per hour. Supercell tornadoes are the type most likely to remain in contact with the ground for an hour or more.

Landspouts aren't as strong as supercell tornadoes. They form from cool, wet air traveling with a thunderstorm. When a landspout's air column touches the ground, it sucks up a layer of dust, giving it another name—dust-tube tornado. This is similar to a waterspout, or a tornado that happens over water. Waterspouts can form from supercell thunderstorms, but they're small and weaken as soon as they hit land.

Tornado "Cousins"

Dust devils are "whirlwinds" that occur in the desert or other very dry areas. These winds swirl dust around but commonly aren't stronger than 70 miles (113 km) per hour. Forest fires or volcanic eruptions can cause "firewhirls." These "firenadoes" may have winds of more than 100 miles (161 km) per hour.

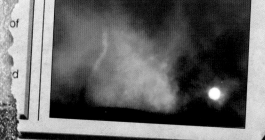

A dust devil is sometimes called a dancing devil or a dust whirl.

▽

waterspout near Sydney, Australia (2010)

FORECASTING

Today, meteorologists know a lot about tornadoes. Some scientists are even experts on the subject. However, many years ago, they didn't have a clear idea about why funnel clouds formed, so it was hard for them to know when a tornado might hit.

In order to predict a tornado today, meteorologists use radar and **satellites** to watch winds all over the country. They find areas in which conditions might cause thunderstorms. Doppler radar allows forecasters to **estimate** wind speeds and watch for mesocyclones. When they see the spinning winds reach a certain formation or speed, they issue a tornado watch.

satellite image of storm system

Doppler Radar

The National Weather Service uses Doppler radar to forecast the weather. "Radar" stands for **RA**dio **D**etection **A**nd **R**anging. Radar sends out radio waves that reflect off things like raindrops. The waves echo back and reveal information about size, shape, and location. Using many of these echoes over a period of time, meteorologists find out how fast a storm is moving.

Doppler radar dishes can be mounted on trucks so they're easily transported to storm locations.

EF SCALE

In the 1970s, the United States started rating tornado **damage** from 0 to 5 on the Fujita Scale, or F Scale. This scale also uses the damage a tornado causes to estimate wind speed.

In 2007, meteorologists adopted the Enhanced Fujita Scale, or EF Scale. It gives more damage indicators than the F Scale and takes into account different kinds and amounts of damage. For example, if the outer walls of a small home fall because of a tornado, damage indicators estimate that the winds were about 132 miles (212 km) per hour. Based on this one indicator, the tornado would rate a 2 on the EF Scale.

Why Do Buildings Fall?

A tornado's winds move at high speeds over a building and pull up. At the same time, the rapidly moving air rushes around the building's corners and pulls out. When the windows and doors break, air rushes in, pushing the walls and roof up. This can happen so quickly it looks as if the building has exploded!

Tornadoes can destroy wind-speed instruments. The EF Scale helps scientists figure out wind speed in miles per hour (MPH).

▼

house destroyed by EF-5 tornado in Joplin, Missouri (2011)

OPERATIONAL EF SCALE

EF NUMBER	3-SECOND GUST
0	65–85 MPH
1	86–110 MPH
2	111–135 MPH
3	136–165 MPH
4	166–200 MPH
5	over 200 MPH

TORNADO OUTBREAKS

A tornado outbreak is the occurrence of many tornadoes in an area, commonly as a result of a thunderstorm system. The tornado Super Outbreak of 2011 was the largest in US history. From April 26 to April 28, more than 300 tornadoes spun across the eastern United States. In the 15 states hit by tornadoes, about 340 people were killed. More than 2,000 people were injured in Alabama alone.

About 2 weeks before this Super Outbreak, 155 tornadoes were reported in several southern states on April 14 and 15. Forty people died during this outbreak.

EF-4 tornado damage in Tuscaloosa, Alabama (2011)

Sometimes, tornadoes last for hours and cause long paths of damage. These are called long-track tornadoes. However, it's hard to prove whether a damage path belongs to just one powerful tornado or a tornado family. These groups usually have two or three tornadoes that form from the same central rotating wind.

Whole communities were destroyed during the Super Outbreak of 2011, including this one in Pleasant Grove, Alabama.

A tornado can be measured by the width of its funnel, the speed of its winds, or the damage it causes. The deadliest tornado in US history was the Tri-State Tornado of 1925. It also set records for length and distance traveled.

The Tri-State Tornado formed March 18, 1925, in Ellington, Missouri. It traveled 219 miles (352 km) through Illinois and Indiana. The winds spun at 300 miles (483 km) per hour, destroying several towns and leaving many people homeless. During its 3½-hour lifetime, the tornado caused 695 deaths and more than 2,000 injuries.

Joplin, Missouri

On May 23, 2011, the worst US tornado in more than 50 years hit Joplin, Missouri. The damage was widespread. Some buildings were ripped right off the ground. More than 150 people died. The Federal Emergency Management Agency (FEMA) was called in to help clean up the debris and rescue those trapped in fallen buildings.

Tri-State Tornado damage in
Griffin, Indiana (1925)

Two young women sit near the
debris of their Illinois home after
the Tri-State Tornado of 1925.

VORTEX

VORTEX—or **V**erification of the **O**rigins of **R**otation in **T**ornadoes **EX**periment—was a large tornado-research project from 1994 to 1995 that explored how, when, and why tornadoes form. However, some of the facts scientists collected just produced more questions.

In 2009, VORTEX 2 became the largest tornado study ever. About 100 scientists used the latest weather instruments to find and track tornadoes. They had trucks outfitted with radar called Doppler on Wheels and tornado pods, which measure wind speed and direction on the ground. One of VORTEX 2's major goals was figuring out how to give communities more warning about tornadoes headed in their direction.

Although storm chasing may seem exciting, it's very dangerous. These men have just minutes to drive to escape the tornado's path.

▼

Storm Chasers

The 1996 movie *Twister* was about scientists who chase tornadoes to study them. Storm chasers don't just exist in movies. There are real-life storm chasers who put themselves in danger! Some are scientists who want to learn more about how weather happens. Some are photographers who want to take pictures of storm scenes as they happen.

tornado researchers with fact-collecting tool

TORNADO SAFETY

The safest place to be during a tornado is in your home's basement. If your home doesn't have a basement, crouch under a sturdy table or take shelter in a room with thick walls and no windows, such as a closet or bathroom. Cover your head with your arms to protect yourself from flying glass or debris.

If you're outside when a tornado hits, find an area of low ground, such as a ditch. Don't stay inside a car or mobile home because tornadoes can be strong enough to turn these over or lift them off the ground.

entrance to underground storm shelter in Oklahoma

Look Up!

Is a tornado about to hit? The sky gives some clues. It becomes dark and a greenish color. A wall cloud may form suddenly and begin to spin. It may hail. Before a tornado starts, you might also hear a load roar like a train is approaching.

This boy practices hiding in a safe place in case a tornado touches down near his school.

GLOSSARY

condense: to lose heat and change from a gas into a liquid

damage: harm. Also, to cause harm.

debris: the remains of something that has been broken down

destructive: causing damage

estimate: a guess based on facts

front: the line between two masses of air

horizontal: level with the line that seems to form where the earth meets the sky

hurricane: a powerful storm that forms over water and causes heavy rainfall and high winds

meteorologist: one who studies Earth's atmosphere, especially to forecast weather

predict: to guess what will happen in the future based on facts or knowledge

rotating: spinning

satellite: an object that circles Earth in order to collect and send information or aid in communication

vertically: in an up-and-down manner

FOR MORE INFORMATION

Books

Adamson, Heather. *Surviving a Tornado*. Mankato, MN: Amicus, 2012.

Dougherty, Terri. *Anatomy of a Tornado*. Mankato, MN: Capstone Press, 2011.

Rudolph, Jessica. *Erased by a Tornado!* New York, NY: Bearport Publishing, 2010.

Websites

Tornadoes
www.fema.gov/kids/tornado.htm
Find out what to do if a tornado hits where you live.

Tornadoes
www.weatherwizkids.com/weather-tornado.htm
Read more about how tornadoes and thunderstorms form.

INDEX